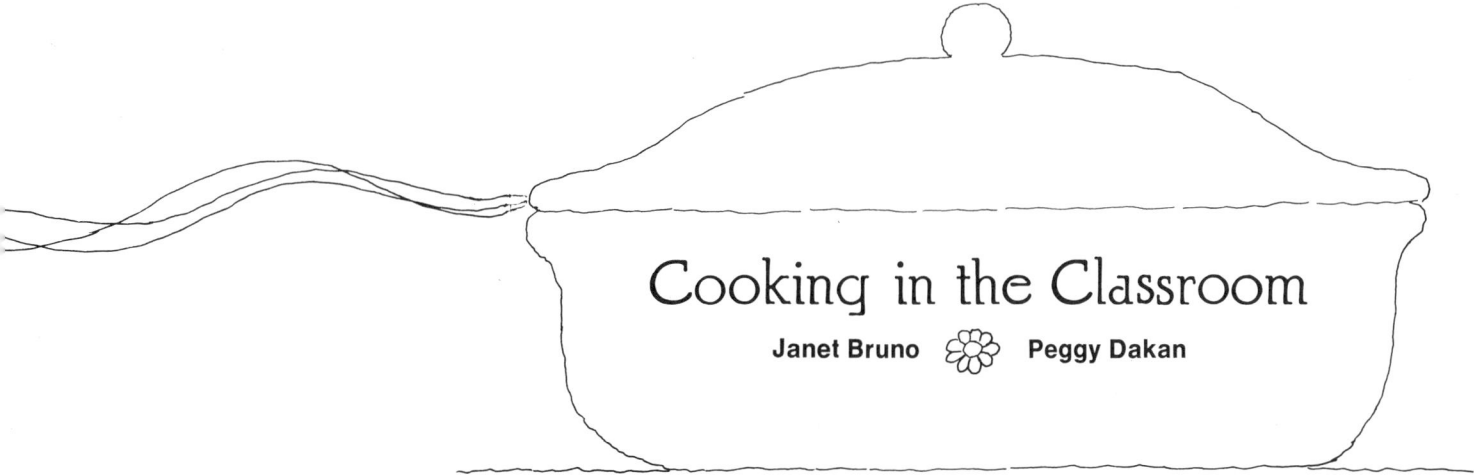

Cooking in the Classroom

Janet Bruno   **Peggy Dakan**

Fearon Teacher Aids
a division of
DAVID S. LAKE PUBLISHERS
Belmont, California

Edited by Lesley Swanson
Designed by Jane Mitchell
Illustrated by Tom Durfee

ISBN-0-8224-1610-7

Printed in the United States of America.

Contents

Preface

It's fun to eat, but it's even more fun to cook what you're going to eat. Not only can you eat the end product, but you can nibble as you work. And there's nothing as thrilling as sharing your tasty creation with family and friends.

Who can forget those happy days from childhood, peeking at cookies bubbling and browning in the oven, smelling the delicious aroma of roast turkey on Thanksgiving Day, or watching Mom bake a cake and licking the frosting left in the bowl.

Children enjoy the same things today, and it's a small step from these happy moments to actually using simple recipes. A love for cooking starts early for both boys and girls when they are allowed to work in the kitchen. The recipes in this book are easy enough to insure success and provide pleasant cooking experiences.

As teachers, we have used cooking in our classrooms and know from experience that children love it. As they work, they learn many skills: how to measure and use fractions, how to spell and use new words, how to follow safety rules. They discover simple science principles, such as how leavening agents work, and what chemical and physical changes occur during cooking. In addition, children develop good work habits such as cleaning up as they go along, completing a task they have started, and following directions carefully.

In this book, we have collected inexpensive, simple recipes that have been "child tested" in our classrooms. We hope these recipes will provide you and your children with many enjoyable learning experiences.

Janet Bruno
Peggy Dakan

Getting Ready to Cook

The recipes and procedures in this book are designed to be used in small groups of one to six students so that each child can actively participate. There are snacks, salads, and main dishes. Each recipe is written in the natural progression for reading development, left to right and top to bottom, with standard pictures to illustrate words and actions. Both picture and recipe pages are addressed to the child, but the helping hands symbol indicates that an adult should assist with that specific task. The *Questions for the Cook* included with each recipe can be used during the cooking experience. They are only suggestions. You may want your cooks to answer all of them, or just one or two. Please do not feel that cooking is only for girls—boys are often more enthusiastic because they've never had a chance to cook.

Before you try recipes that require extensive measuring, it's wise to provide several measuring experiences as part of your math curriculum. Show the class the correct way to use both dry and liquid measuring utensils, then set out the equipment at the cooking center so each child can have a chance to practice. Cooking is a great way to introduce fractions. You might write job cards that require experimentation, such as:

Use your measuring spoons to find out:

1 T. = _____tsp.
1 tsp. = _____½ tsp.
½ tsp. = _____¼ tsp.

Look at the ingredients on this table.

(milk, sugar, salt, water, soda, flour, pepper, vanilla, spices, rice, raisins)

On a piece of paper, list the ingredients and tell what measuring utensils you would probably use for each one.

(water—glass measuring cup)

When you feel that the class is ready to begin cooking, follow this procedure:

1. Provide a comfortable working space that is child-sized.
2. Read through the recipe together. Decide what you need and gather all the materials. You might even take a field trip and do the marketing together.
3. Go over the safety rules together.
4. Discuss the Word List at the bottom of each recipe page.
5. Read one line of the recipe at a time and perform the indicated operations. Let the children do as much as possible on their own.
6. Clean up as you go along. This is the children's responsibility. You might set up two dishpans, one for washing and one for rinsing.
7. If you are going to eat right away, the children can set the table with appropriate tableware. You may need a complete place setting or perhaps just napkins, depending upon the recipe.
8. Sampling the finished product is part of the evaluation. This is also the time to develop vocabulary: "How did it taste? Was it tart or sweet? Creamy or crumbly?" In addition, you will need to evaluate the total experience: "What went well today? What problems did you have? Did everyone share in the work?"

Cooking Partners. If you teach older children, you might want to use a more independent approach by letting each child choose a cooking partner. In this case, you'll need to design a cooking schedule that lets them use the center two at a time. In addition to following the recipes by themselves, pairs of older children can use job cards such as these as a follow up to the cooking experience:

Divide a piece of paper into three columns. List 5 sweet foods in the first column; 5 tart foods in the second; and 5 sour foods in the third.

Make a collage using pictures of fruits or vegetables cut from magazines.

Write a recipe for Carrot and Apple Salad that would give you *double* the amount of salad.

Find out and explain to the class why lemon juice prevents some fruits from turning brown.

Table Setting. Depending on the level of your class, you might want to try one or more of the following activities:

- Deposit a variety of silverware, plates, napkins, and glasses at the cooking center. Let the children practice setting a table for four.
- Make and decorate paper placemats. Paste pictures of dinner plates, silverware, salad plates, glasses, and napkins on the placemats.
- Make name cards to take home for a family dinner.
- Arrange a centerpiece using dried flowers and weeds, fruits, gourds, or candles.
- Create a centerpiece for a special occasion (birthday, holiday).

Nutrition. To help children become aware of the four basic food groups (dairy products; meats, beans, nuts; fruits and vegetables; breads and cereals) here are some activities that could either be written on job cards or used with the class as a whole.

1. Keep track of the foods you eat for one week. Draw a chart showing which food groups they belong to.
2. Use your Nutrition Wheel to help you plan a balanced menu for breakfast, lunch, and dinner.
3. Make a calorie count of one of your meals.
4. Use magazine pictures to make a food collage of one or all four food groups.
5. Create a balanced meal on a paper plate using magazine pictures or modeling clay.
6. Make a chart showing all the foods made from one basic food such as corn.
7. Use supermarket ads cut out of the daily newspaper to do the following activity: "Find out how much money the average American family spends on food each week. Assume you have that amount of money to buy groceries for your family for one week. You must include four items from each of the four basic food groups. Write down your grocery list. Be sure to take advantage of sale items."

8. Take a walking trip to your local supermarket. Make a list of the food items that are displayed at the ends of the aisles. Why are they placed there? List 30 packaged foods you see. From which basic food is each one made?

NUTRITION WHEEL. Draw four circles, 6″, 5″, 4″, and 3″ in diameter respectively. Ditto each wheel on a different color construction paper. Let the children cut out the four circles and assemble them (smallest one on top) with a paper fastener. Have them label the bottom wheel *breads* and *cereals*, the next one *fruits* and *vegetables*, the third one *eggs*, *beans*, and *meat* or *fish*, and the top one *milk*.

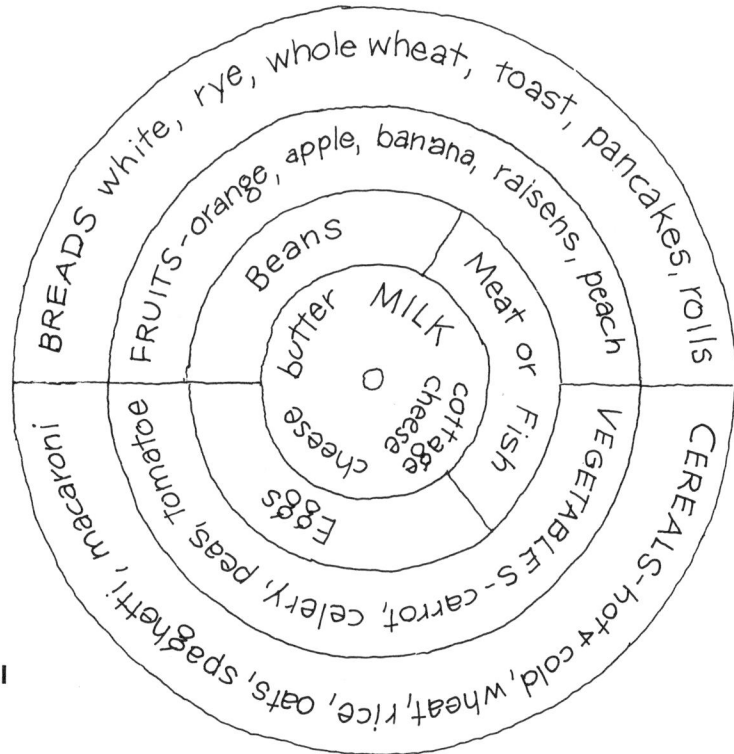

Nutrition Wheel

Key to Symbols

Helping Hand. This is the helping hand symbol. It means that you should ask the teacher to help you with this part of the recipe.

Preheat Oven. Some of the foods in this book need to be baked in the oven. This dial will remind you to preheat the oven to the correct temperature before you begin mixing the ingredients.

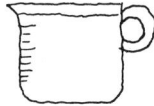

Measure 1 cup

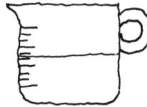

Measure ½ cup

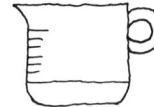

Measure ¼ cup

Measure 1 tablespoon

Measure 1 teaspoon

Measure ½ teaspoon

Dash

Measure ¼ teaspoon

Safety Tips

1. Always wash hands before handling food.
2. Things that are hot don't always look hot. If you get a burn, immediately hold the burned area under cold running water.
3. Always use a dry potholder to lift pans out of the oven, never a wet one.
4. When chopping, cutting, or peeling food, use a cutting board. Cut away from yourself, and keep your fingers away from the blade.
5. Keep pot handles on the stove turned away from you.
6. Turn the burner or oven off before removing pans.
7. Stand mixing bowls in the sink as you stir—its saves splashes.
8. Use hand beaters, a large spoon, or a wire whip instead of electric beaters. This way, you have a chance to get the feel of the batter.

Peanut Butter Balls

Makes 1 dozen

UTENSILS

mixing bowl
large spoon
liquid measuring cup
dry measuring cup

INGREDIENTS

1 cup peanut butter
1 cup honey
1½ cups powdered milk

Questions for the Cook

1. What is powdered milk? Why don't we use regular milk in this recipe?
2. Why don't we cook this recipe?
3. Find out how peanut butter is made.
4. Find out how much of each ingredient we would need to double the recipe.
5. Roll a cookie on a plate. Then roll one on waxed paper. Which way do you think works best?
6. Where does honey come from?

Word List: powdered, liquid, dry

Peanut Butter Balls

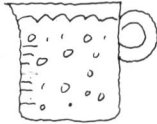

Measure   1 cup peanut butter.

1 cup honey.

Mix in bowl.

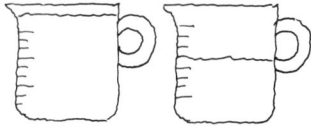

Add   1½ cups powdered milk. Stir.

Roll into little balls. Share with many friends.

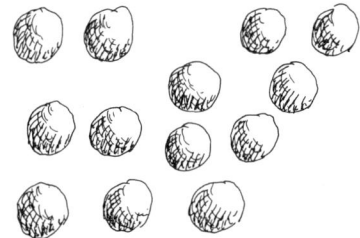

Full O'Baloney Animals

Serves 1

UTENSILS
cookie cutter
knife

INGREDIENTS
2 slices bread
1 slice baloney
butter
apple
milk

Questions for the Cook

1. What other food do you think we could put in this sandwich?
2. Try making this sandwich with special cookie cutters for holidays.
3. What other foods can you cut with a cookie cutter? Try cutting a piece of lettuce or a slice of cheese.
4. Find out what foods baloney is made from.

Word List: between, baloney

Full O'Baloney Animals

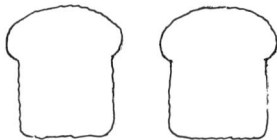

Butter 2 slices bread. **Add** 1 slice baloney.

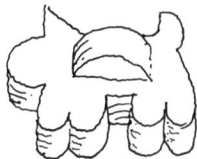

Use cookie cutter. Press hard.

**Put animal on plate.
Serve with apple and milk.**

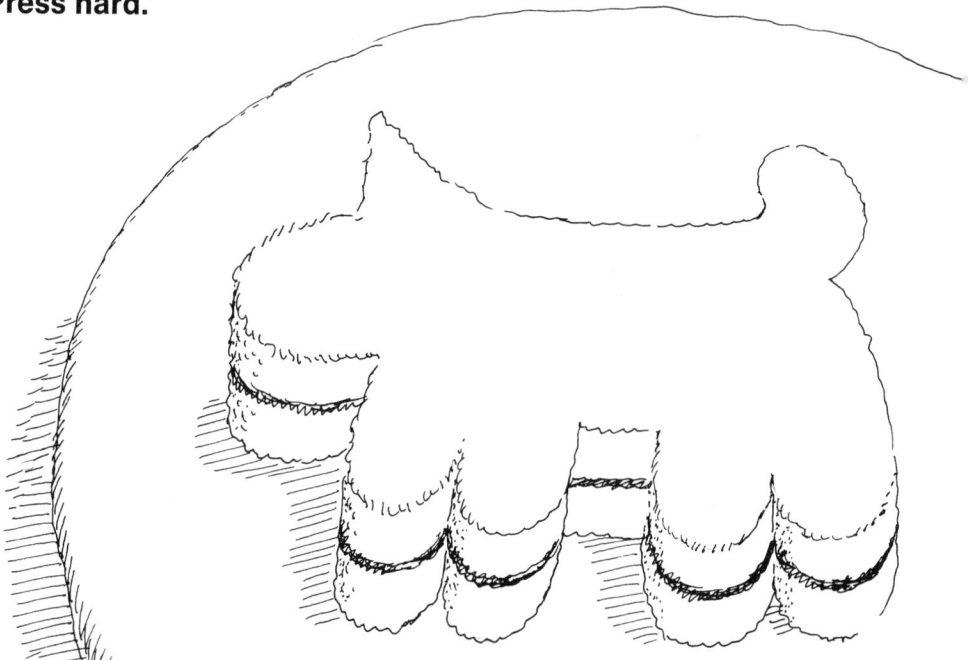

Fruit Tree Salad

Serves 1

UTENSILS

plate
can opener
toothpicks
strainer

INGREDIENTS

lettuce
1 slice pineapple
banana
1 small can fruit cocktail

Questions for the Cook

1. Why do you think it is important to wash the lettuce before we eat it?
2. Compare a canned pineapple slice with some fresh pineapple. Do they taste, smell, or look the same? How are they different?
3. Think of other salads you could make using fruit. Draw a picture of one. Label each kind of fruit you use.
4. Find out what kinds of fruit are in the fruit cocktail.

Word List: leaf, slice, strainer

Fruit Tree Salad

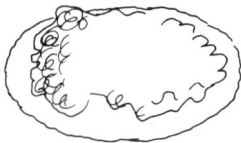

Put on plate   1 lettuce leaf.

Put in center   1 slice pineapple.

Put in hole   ½ peeled banana.

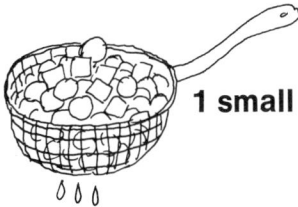

Drain   1 small can fruit cocktail.

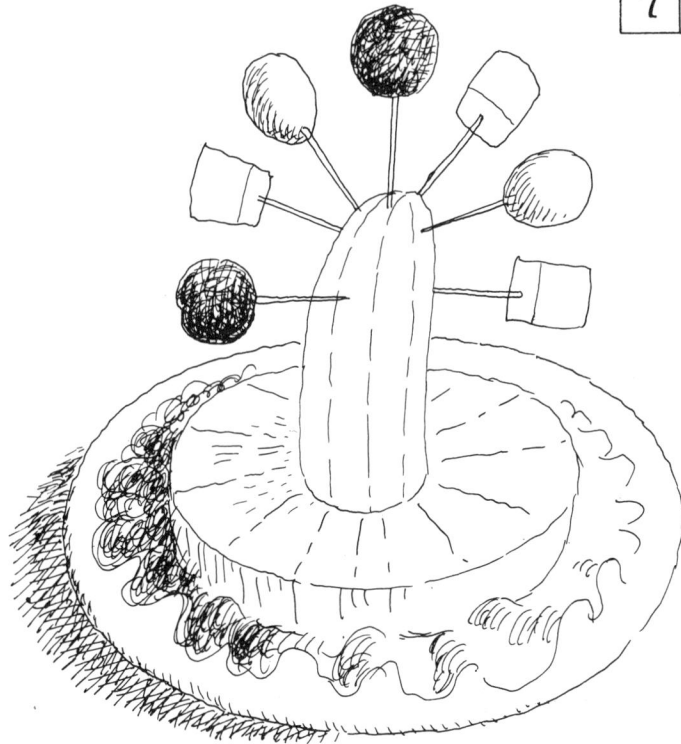

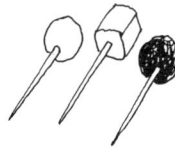

Put toothpicks through fruit.
Put fruit on banana.

Shake-a-Puddin'

Serves 2 or 3

UTENSILS

plastic container with lid
liquid measuring cup
small bowls or paper cups

INGREDIENTS

1 small box instant pudding, any flavor
2 c. milk

Questions for the Cook

1. Taste a little bit of the dry pudding. Can you tell what flavor it will be? Count out loud as you shake it.
2. How does the mixture change in color and feel when it has set?
3. Write down five words that tell how the pudding feels and tastes.
4. Try finger painting with some pudding.

Word List: instant, pudding

Shake-a-Puddin'

Put in shaker  **1 small package instant pudding.**

Add: 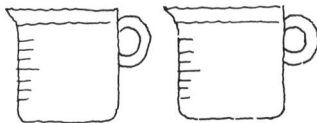 **2 cups milk.**

Put top on tightly. Shake  **20 times.**

Pour into dishes.
Count slowly to 20.
Then eat!

Mellow Yellow

Serves 2

UTENSILS
frying pan
spatula
knife

INGREDIENTS
butter
cheese
bread

Questions for the Cook
1. Why do you think we butter the bread?
2. How does the bread change when it is heated? What happens to the cheese?
3. What Happens if you leave the sandwich in the pan to long? Let a small piece of bread continue to cook after you take the sandwich out. What happens to it? About how long does the sandwich need to cook? Time it.
4. Next time you are in a grocery store, look at the cheeses. Can you name *five* different kinds of cheese?

Word List: triangle, spatula

Mellow Yellow

Butter: 2 slices Bread.

Add: 1 slice cheese.

Measure 1 tablespoon butter. **Melt in pan.**

Brown bread on both sides.

**Cut into triangles.
Share with a friend.**

Celery and Pineapple Sticks

Serves 12

UTENSILS
knife
bowl
large spoon
strainer
tray

INGREDIENTS
6 stalks celery
8-ounce package cream cheese
1 small can crushed pineapple

Questions for the Cook

1. How is cream cheese different from regular cheese?
2. What else can you think of that might be good for stuffing celery?
3. Make a design with the celery on the tray. Why do you think it is important to fix the celery so it looks nice?
4. What part of the celery plant do we eat?

Word List: stalk, crushed, half, to mash, to drain

Celery and Pineapple Sticks

Cut in half   **6 stalks celery. Mash**   **1 8-ounce package cream cheese.**

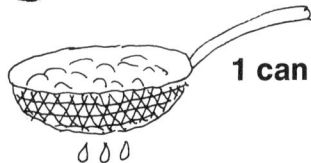

Drain   **1 can crushed pineapple.**

Mix pineapple and cream cheese.

Put mixture in celery. Put celery on tray.

Dough Dolls

Serves 1 class

UTENSILS
cookie sheet
pastry brush

INGREDIENTS
1 loaf frozen bread dough
1 egg white

Questions for the Cook

1. How does the dough feel when it's frozen? When it's defrosted?
2. Taste a little piece. Is it ready to eat?
3. Draw a picture of the shape you made with the dough. Draw another picture of it when it is ready to bake. What is the difference?
4. Taste a little piece of the dough before you put it in the oven. Is it ready to eat yet?
5. Find out what yeast is. What does it do to the bread dough?

Word List: to defrost, to double, yeast

Dough Dolls

325°

Defrost 1 loaf frozen bread dough.

Roll dough in a ball.

Pat dough out.

On a greased cookie sheet, make any shape you want. Let rise in warm place until double in size. Then brush with egg white. Bake until golden brown.

Hot Chocolate Mix

Makes a lot

UTENSILS

mixing bowl
large spoon
measuring spoon
drinking cups
airtight container

INGREDIENTS

1 pound Nestles Quik
1 pound powdered sugar
1 6-ounce jar instant cream
1 8-quart box instant non-fat milk
hot water

Questions for the Cook

1. Compare powdered sugar and granulated sugar. Do they look the same? Do they taste the same? Do they feel the same?
2. Why do you think we use instant cream and milk in this recipe instead of fresh cream and milk?
3. Find out how many ounces there are in a pound.
4. Find out how you can make your own powdered sugar.
5. What is the difference between non-fat milk and whole milk? What is buttermilk?

Word List: pound, ounce, quart, airtight

Hot Chocolate Mix

Mix   1 pound instant chocolate drink,   1 pound powdered sugar,

1 6-ounce jar instant cream,   1 8-quart box instant non-fat milk.

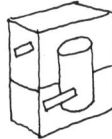

Keep in airtight container.

Put 3 tablespoons mix in 1 cup hot water Stir and enjoy!

Toad-in-a Hole

Serves 1

UTENSILS

cookie cutter
knife
spatula
frying pan with lid
measuring spoons

INGREDIENTS

1 slice bread
1 egg
1 tablespoon butter

Questions for the Cook

1. What happens to butter when it is heated? What happens if you let the butter bubble for one minute? Two minutes? When is it best to put the egg in?
2. Why do we put butter in the pan?
3. How does the egg change as it cooks?
4. Can you think of four other ways to cook an egg?

Word List: to jiggle, to brown

Toad-in-a Hole

Butter both sides of 1 slice bread.

Use cookie cutter. Cut out center of bread.

Melt in pan 1 tablespoon butter.

Brown bread on both sides.

Break into hole 1 egg.

Cook covered until
egg doesn't jiggle.

Bunny Salad

Serves 1

UTENSILS

plate
knife

INGREDIENTS

lettuce
1 orange
1 canned pear half
1 maraschino cherry

Questions for the Cook

1. What is the difference between canned and fresh fruit? Do you think they taste different? Find out what climate pears grow best in.
2. Try making this salad again. Use the same ingredients but make another animal.
3. Are any of these ingredients cooked?

Word List: to decorate, section, maraschino

Bunny Salad

Put on plate   1 lettuce leaf.

Put cut side down   1 canned pear half.

Add   4 sections orange for ears.

Cut into 6 slices   1 maraschino cherry,
Add eyes, nose, mouth
and inside of ears.

Olive and Cheese Snacks

Serves 12

UTENSILS
knife
toothpicks
tray

INGREDIENTS
1 small jar stuffed green olives
1 small brick cheese
parsley

Questions for the Cook

1. Find out how many calories there are in ten green olives and in one ounce of cheese.
   Find out how many calories there are in one piece of frosted chocolate cake.
2. Why do you think this kind of snack is better for you than candy or cookies?
3. Can you think of other nutritious snack foods? Write down four of them.
4. Why do you think we put parsley on the tray?

Word List: stuffed, to decorate, cube

Olive and Cheese Snacks

Cut in half 25 stuffed green olives.

Cut in cubes 1 small brick cheese.

Put on toothpick 1 cube cheese and ½ olive.

Cut leaves off 1 bunch parsley.

Put snacks on tray.
Decorate with parsley.

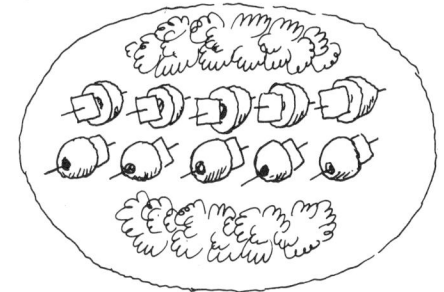

Dip-it-e-do

Serves 8

UTENSILS

knife
toothpicks
saucepan

INGREDIENTS

4 bananas
1 6-ounce package semi-sweet chocolate chips
½ cup chopped peanuts

Questions for the Cook

1. Look closely at the banana slices. What do you see in the center?
2. What happens to the chocolate bits when you heat them?
3. What happens to the chocolate as it cools on the banana?
4. Try dipping the chocolate-covered banana into coconut flakes.
   What else could you dip it in?
5. Try dipping other fruit (apples, oranges, pineapples) into the chocolate
   Which one do you like best?

Word List: fourths, semi-sweet, to peel

Dip-it-e-do

Peel 4 bananas.   Cut in fourths.

Put toothpicks through bananas.

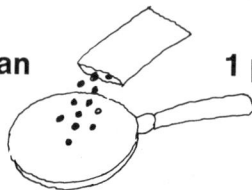

Melt in pan   1 package chocolate chips.

Dip banana in chocolate.

Roll in peanuts.

Campfire Beans

Serves 8

UTENSILS

large spoon
1½ quart casserole
measuring spoons
liquid measuring cup

INGREDIENTS

2 large cans barbecue beans
¼ cup light molasses
1 teaspoon Worcestershire sauce
2 tablespoons prepared mustard

Questions for the Cook

1. Taste a little bit of molasses. Find out where it comes from.
2. How do the ingredients smell before they are baked? After they are baked?
3. What happens to the molasses when the beans are cooked?
4. Why do you think we call them barbecue beans?

Word List: barbecue, molasses, Worcestershire sauce, casserole

Campfire Beans 350°

Open BEANS BEANS **2 large cans barbecue beans. Pour into casserole.**

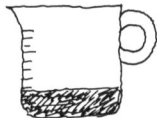

Add ¼ **cup molasses,** **2 tablespoons mustard,**

1 teaspoon Worcestershire sauce. Stir well. **Bake uncovered 30 minutes.**

One Cup Salad

Serves 5

UTENSILS

mixing bowl
large spoon
dry measuring cups
can opener
knife

INGREDIENTS

1 cup diced bananas
1 cup fruit cocktail
1 cup tiny marshmallows
1 cup crushed pineapple
1 cup sour cream

Questions for the Cook

1. If we wanted to make only half this recipe, how much of each ingredient would we need?
2. What is the difference between regular cream and sour cream? Describe how each one tastes and feels.
3. Find out how sour cream is made.

Word List: diced, cocktail

One Cup Salad

Measure  1 cup diced bananas.

 1 cup fruit cocktail.

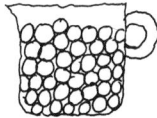 1 cup tiny marshmallows.

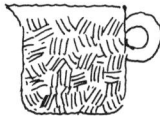 1 cup crushed pineapple.

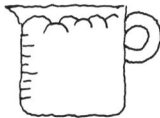 1 cup sour cream.

Mix and chill.

French Toast

Serves 1

UTENSILS

mixing bowl
measuring spoons
fork
knife
spatula
frying pan

INGREDIENTS

1 egg
1 tablespoon milk
1 slice bread
1 tablespoon butter
granulated sugar
syrup

Questions for the Cook

1. How is the bread like a sponge?
2. Does the bread change color as it cooks? Why?
3. What is the difference between granulated and powdered sugar? Taste a little
   bit of each kind. Do they taste the same or different?

Word List: to sprinkle, granulated

French Toast

Put in bowl 1 egg and 1 tablespoon milk. Beat with fork.

Take 1 slice bread. Dip on both sides.

Measure 1 tablespoon butter. Melt in pan.

Brown bread on both sides.

Sprinkle with 1 teaspoon sugar.

Serve with butter and syrup.

ABC Soup

Serves 6

UTENSILS
kettle
liquid measuring cup
dry measuring cup
large spoon
can opener
knife
ladle

INGREDIENTS
4 cups beef bouillon
½ cup diced potato
½ cup diced celery
½ cup diced carrot
½ cup diced onion
1 cup alphabet noodles

Questions for the Cook

1. How do the alphabet noodles change after they have been cooked?
2. Before adding the noodles, try to find all the letters in the alphabet. Can you spell your name with them? How many other words can you spell?
3. For variety, use different vegetables. How will the recipe change if you add leafy vegetables that have a short cooking time?
4. Read the story "Stone Soup." Make this recipe into "stone soup" by adding a special stone that you have found.

Word List: bouillon, kettle

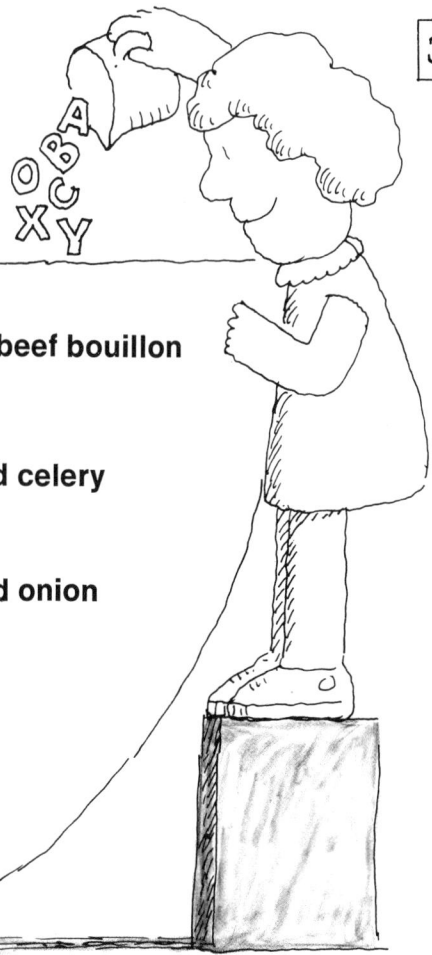

ABC Soup

Measure 4 cups beef bouillon

½ cup diced potato   ½ cup diced celery

½ cup diced carrot   ¼ cup diced onion

Put in large kettle. Cover and simmer 30 minutes.

Add 1 cup alphabet noodles.

Cook 5 more minutes.

Peanut Crispies

Makes 1 dozen

UTENSILS

**saucepan
large spoon
waxed paper
liquid measuring cup
dry measuring cup
teaspoons**

INGREDIENTS

**½ cup Karo syrup
½ cup sugar
1 cup peanut butter
1 cup chow mein noodles**

Questions for the Cook

1. How can you tell when the syrup and sugar boil?
2. What happens to the mixture when it cools?
3. Use a candy thermometer to find the boiling temperature of the syrup and sugar.
   What is the boiling temperature of water?
4. Find out how you can make your own peanut butter.

Word List: chow mein, noodle, to boil

Peanut Crispies

Measure ½ cup sugar.

½ cup Karo syrup.

Stir and bring to boil.

Measure 1 cup peanut butter.

1 cup chow mein noodles.

Take pan off stove and stir in.

Drop by spoon on wax paper.

Cool. Share with a friend.

Cheesy Beans

Serves 8

UTENSILS

kettle with lid
large spoon
frying pan
knife
fork
grater

INGREDIENTS

2 cups dry pinto beans
1 onion
2 teaspoons salt
1 cup grated cheese
1 tablespoon butter
water

Questions for the Cook

1. Why do you think we need to sort and wash the beans?
2. Measure the beans when they are cooked. How many cups are there now?
3. Find out what food value there is in dry beans. How do they compare with meat?
4. What happens to the water as the beans cook?
5. Put some dry beans in a pan and cover them with cold water. Let them stand overnight. What do they look like the next day? Are they ready to eat?

Word List: to mash, to grate, to sort

Cheesy Beans

Measure 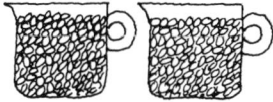 2 cups beans. Sort and wash in kettle.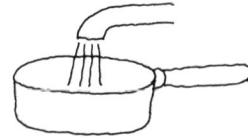

Add 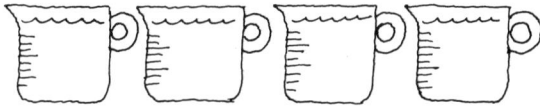 4 cups water,  2 teaspoons salt.

Cover and simmer 3 hours or until soft.
Add more water if necessary.

Chop  1 onion. Put in hot pan with  1 tablespoon butter.

Add beans. Mash. **Grate 1 cup cheese.**
Sprinkle over beans and eat.

Finger Jell-o

Makes a lot

UTENSILS

mixing bowls
liquid measuring cup
dry measuring cup
large spoon
8″ square pan
knife
measuring spoons

INGREDIENTS

4 envelopes unflavored gelatin
1 cup sugar
3 small packages Jell-o
1 tablespoon lemon juice
water

Questions for the Cook

1. Does the gelatin dissolve faster if you stir it, or if you leave it alone? Which dissolves faster, the sugar and the Jell-o, or the unflavored gelatin? Time them.
2. How does the unflavored gelatin smell? How does the Jell-o smell?
3. How does the Jell-o feel when you pour it in the pan? How does it feel when it's ready to eat? Write down five words that describe the way it feels.
4. Try adding fruit, marshmallows, or nuts to the Jell-o.
5. Try making double-decker Jell-o by making one pan and letting it cool, then pouring another flavor on top.

Word List: gelatin, to dissolve, square, to chill

Finger Jell-o

Put in bowl 4 envelopes gelatin. **Dissolve in 2 cups water.**

Put in another bowl 1 cup sugar,

3 small packages Jell-o

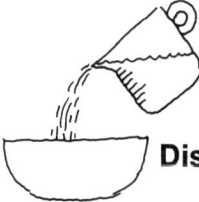

Dissolve in 3 cups hot water.

Add 1 tablespoon lemon juice.

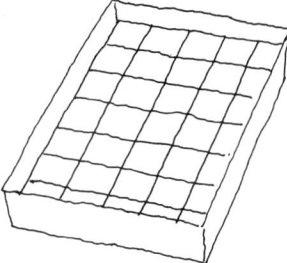

Pour contents of both bowls into square pan. Chill Cut into squares.

April Fools Ice Cream Cones

Serves 10

UTENSILS

mixing bowl
large spoon
cookie sheet
knife
can opener

INGREDIENTS

1 packaged cake mix, any flavor
10 flat-bottom ice cream cones
1 can prepared frosting

Questions for the Cook

1. Without reading the directions on the package, guess what ingredients you will have to add to the cake mix. Write them down. Now read the directions. What ingredients did you forget? Write them down.
2. Choose one cone to watch as it bakes. Draw a picure of the way it looks when you put it in the oven. Draw one picture of it after 10 minutes and another picture after 20 minutes.
3. How did the cake mix change in size? In texture? In smell?
4. Did the cones change?
5. Why do you think the cones need to cool before they are frosted? Try frosting one that is hot out of the oven. What happens?

Word List: to frost, ingredients

April Fools Ice Cream Cones

350°

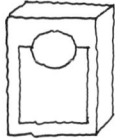

Mix   Any cake mix by package directions.

Fill ½ full   10 flat bottom ice cream cones.

Bake on cookie sheet 25 minutes.

Frost with 1 can frosting, strawberry or chocolate.

Carrot and Apple Salad

Serves 3

UTENSILS
vegetable peeler
grater
salad bowl
large spoon
dry measuring cups
measuring spoons

INGREDIENTS
1 carrot
2 apples
½ cup raisins
⅓ cup mayonnaise
1 teaspoon lemon juice

Questions for the Cook

1. Why do we add lemon juice to this salad? Cut and peel two slices of an apple.
   Put them on a plate. Pour lemon juice over one slice, and leave the other one plain.
   Look at them after an hour. Do you see any change?
2. Why do we mix this salad gently?
3. How would you describe the taste? Is it sweet? Sour? Tart?
4. Find out what ingredients go into mayonnaise.

Word List: mayonnaise, peeler

Carrot and Apple Salad

 **Peel**  **1 carrot**  **2 apples.**

Grate carrot and apples in bowl.

Add  **½ cup raisins,**

 **⅓ cup mayonnaise,**

 **1 teaspoon lemon juice.**

Mix gently.

Kooky Cookies

Makes 2 dozen

UTENSILS

mixing bowl
large spoon
teaspoons
cookie sheet
liquid measuring cup
measuring spoons
spatula

INGREDIENTS

1 packaged cake mix, any flavor
½ cup oil
2 tablespoons water
2 eggs
½ cup nuts or chocolate chips

Questions for the Cook

1. Count out loud as you stir the batter. How many times did you stir it?
2. Why do we need to drop the cookies far apart on the cookie sheet? Try putting two cookies very close together. What happens?
3. Try to make exactly two dozen cookies.
4. Draw a picture of a cookie before it is baked and after it is baked. How does the batter change?
5. How is a measuring teaspoon different from the teaspoon you eat with?

Word List: dozen, spatula

Kooky Cookies

350°

Mix 1 package cake mix, ½ cup oil, 2 tablespoons water, 2 eggs

Add ½ cup nuts or chocolate chips.

Drop by teaspoon on ungreased cookie sheet. Bake 10-12 minutes.

Tooty Fruity

Serves 16

UTENSILS

rolling pin
small saucepan
mixing bowl
large spoon
grater
dry measuring cup
liquid measuring cup
8″ square pan
knife

INGREDIENTS

1 cup zwieback crumbs
¼ cup butter
¼ cup Karo syrup
1 orange
½ cup raisins

Questions for the Cook

1. What does the syrup do to the dry crumbs?
2. Find out what fruit raisins come from.
3. Why do the cookies have to sit overnight?
4. What is the rind of an orange? What other fruits have a rind?

Word List: rind, syrup, to press, zwieback

Tooty Fruity

Roll into crumbs 1 cup zwieback biscuits.

Melt ¼ cup butter, ¼ cup Karo syrup.

Stir crumbs, butter, and syrup.

Add grated rind of 1 orange, ½ cup raisins.

Press into greased pan.
Leave overnight. Cut into bars.

Rice Pudding

Serves 6

UTENSILS

1½ quart casserole
measuring spoons
dry measuring cups
pot holders
liquid measuring cups

INGREDIENTS

½ cup rice
½ cup sugar
4 cups milk
½ teaspoon salt
1 teaspoon lemon peel
¼ teaspoon nutmeg
½ cup raisins

Questions for the Cook

1. Why do we grease the casserole dish?
2. How does the rice change when it is cooked?
3. What happens to the milk after baking?
4. Taste a little bit of nutmeg and lemon peel. Why do you think we add these to the rice?

Word List: to grease, nutmeg

Rice Pudding  300°

Measure 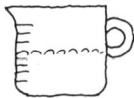 ½ **cup rice,** 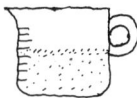 ½ **cup sugar,** 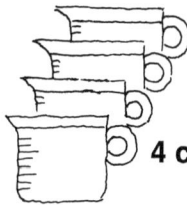 **4 cups milk,** ½ **teaspoon salt.**

Put in greased casserole. **Bake 1 hour.** 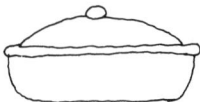 **Take out of oven.**

Add  **1 teaspoon lemon peel,**

¼ teaspoon nutmeg,

½ cup raisins.

Bake 2 more hours.

Angel Cakes

Serves 6

UTENSILS

mixing bowl
large spoon
dry measuring cup
liquid measuring cup
muffin tin

INGREDIENTS

1 cup flour
½ cup liquid shortening
½ cup sugar
1 egg
milk

Questions for the Cook

1. Be sure to measure the flour correctly. Fill the measuring cup, then level it with a knife.
2. Is it easy to mix the shortening into the flour? How long did it take you?
3. How does the batter look, feel, and taste before it bakes? Write down three words that describe it.
4. Draw a picture of the way the muffin tin looks when you put it in the oven. Draw another picture of it when you take it out. How are they different?

Word List: golden, shortening, to level

Angel Cakes

 350°

Measure 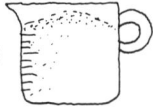 1 cup flour,

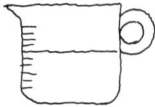 ½ cup liquid shortening.

Mix in bowl

Stir in 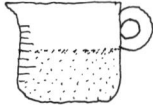 ½ cup sugar, 1 egg, and a little bit of milk.

Spoon into a greased muffin tin. Bake until golden.

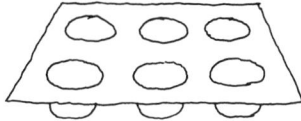

51

Pink Rice

Serves 4

UTENSILS

**dry measuring cup
liquid measuring cup
large spoon
saucepan with lid
measuring spoons
knife**

INGREDIENTS

**1 cup rice
3 tablespoons margarine
¼ cup chopped onion
½ cup tomato sauce
1½ cups water
½ teaspoon salt
¼ teaspoon pepper**

Questions for the Cook

1. Put a mark on the outside of the pan level with the rice.
   After the rice has cooked and the pan has cooled,
   put another mark on the pan level with the rice. How much
   did the rice expand? Measure the difference with a ruler.
2. Find out about different kinds of rice.
3. Find out how rice is grown and harvested.
4. Find out what an onion plant looks like. Draw a picture of it.
   How could you grow an onion plant?
5. Why do some people's eyes water when they are near a raw, cut onion?

Word List: to simmer, to expand

Pink Rice

Measure 1 cup rice, ¼ cup chopped onion.

Brown in 3 tablespoons butter

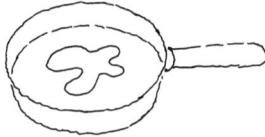

Add and stir 1½ cup water,

½ cup tomato sauce,

½ teaspoon salt, ¼ teaspoon pepper.

Cover and simmer 25 — 30 minutes.

PINK IS BEAUTIFUL

Porcupine Balls

Serves 4–6

UTENSILS

mixing bowl
large spoon
frying pan with lid
liquid measuring cup
measuring spoons
can opener

INGREDIENTS

1½ pounds ground beef
½ cup cooked rice
1 teaspoon salt
¼ teaspoon pepper
1 10-ounce can condensed tomato soup
½ cup water

Questions for the Cook

1. How does the raw meat and rice mixture feel?
   Taste a piece of uncooked rice.
2. Do the porcupine balls change in size as they cook?
3. Does the amout of liquid change as it cooks?
4. Taste a piece of cooked rice. How is it different from the uncooked rice?
5. As the meat simmers, hold a pie plate over the frying pan. After a few minutes, you will see drops of water forming on the plate. Where do they come from?
6. Find out what a porcupine looks like. Why do you think this recipe is called porcupine balls?

Word List: condensed, porcupine

Porcupine Balls

Mix together 1½ pounds ground beef, **Roll into balls.**

½ cup cooked rice,

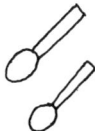

1 teaspoon salt,

½ teaspoon pepper.

Heat in pan 1 10-ounce can condensed tomato soup,

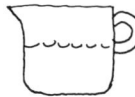

½ cup water.

Simmer meat in sauce for 30 minutes.

Giant Creeping Pancake

Serves 6

UTENSILS

**dry measuring cups
measuring spoons
10″–12″ ovenproof skillet
large spoon
fork or egg beater
mixing bowl**

INGREDIENTS

**½ cup flour
½ cup milk
2 eggs
6 tablespoons margarine
dash nutmeg
2 tablespoons lemon juice
powdered sugar**

Questions for the Cook

1. Watch the batter as it cooks. How does it change? Why do you think it does this?
2. Find out where nutmeg comes from.
3. Find out what a leavening agent is. What is the leavening agent in this recipe?

Word List: skillet, ovenproof, dash

Giant Creeping Pancake

425° *(Put skillet in oven to heat to 425°).*

Beat in bowl 2 eggs. Add

½ cup flour,

½ cup milk,

dash of nutmeg.

Beat well.

Measure 6 tablespoons butter. Melt in hot skillet.

Pour batter into skillet. Bake 15 minutes.

Sprinkle with powdered sugar and lemon juice. Bake 5 more minutes.

Three Green Salad

Serves 6

UTENSILS

salad bowl
knife
liquid measuring cup
measuring spoons
salad servers

INGREDIENTS

romaine
spinach
chicory
2 tomatoes
2 stalks of celery
½ cup salad oil
2 tablespoons vinegar
sugar
salt

Questions for the Cook

1. Which ingredients are crisp? Which ones are soft?
2. How do the greens look alike? How do they look different?
   Draw and label each leafy vegetable.
3. Which ingredients add color to the salad?
4. What other ingredients do you think could be added?
5. Taste each of the dressing ingredients before you mix them.
   Do you think they taste better separate or mixed?
6. How does the salad dressing feel? Write down three words that describe it.

Word List: chunks, greens, wedges, to toss

Three Green Salad

Wash ½ head romaine,
½ bunch spinach,
4 leaves chicory.

Tear in a large bowl.

Cut in wedges 2 large tomatoes.

Cut in chunks 2 stalks celery.

Measure ½ cup oil,

2 tablespoons vinegar,

Pinch of sugar,

Dash of salt.

Toss lightly with dressing.

Cheese Puff 'n Stuff

Serves 6

UTENSILS

mixing bowl
large spoon
1½ quart casserole
knife
teaspoon
measuring spoons
liquid measuring cup
dry measuring cup

INGREDIENTS

6 slices bread
2½ cups diced cheese
butter
3 eggs
2½ cups milk
1 teaspoon salt
¼ teaspoon prepared mustard

Questions for the Cook

1. How does the egg and milk mixture change when it is beaten?
2. Why do we dice the cheese? Could we grate it instead?
3. How does baking change the ingredients? What makes this food rise?
4. How many tablespoons of butter did you use to butter the bread?

Word List: to alternate, quart, layer, prepared mustard

Cheese Puff 'n Stuff

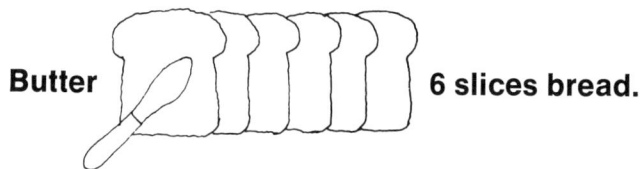

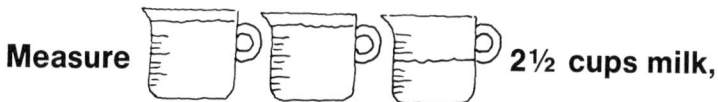

325°

Butter 6 slices bread.

Measure 2½ cups diced cheese.

Measure 2½ cups milk,

3 eggs, 1 teaspoon salt, ¼ teaspoon mustard.

Alternate layers of cheese and bread in greased casserole.

Beat together.

Pour mixture into casserole.
Bake 30 — 45 minutes until
knife comes out clean.

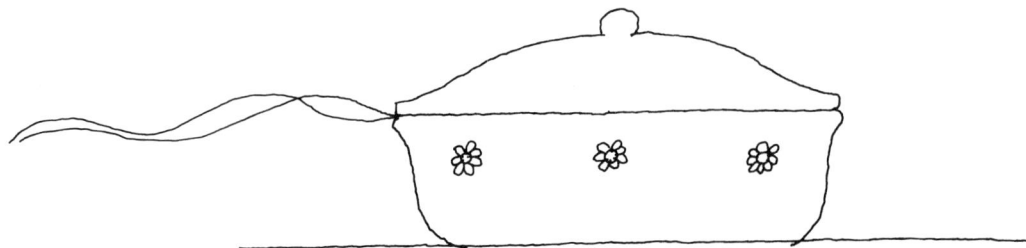

We hope these recipes have provided you and your children
with many enjoyable learning experiences.